two-headed woman

two-headed woman

by lucille clifton

university of massachusetts

press

amherst, 1980

Some of the poems in this collection have
previously been published:
"what the mirror said," "my friends," and "for the mute"
in *American Rag* (fall 1978);
"there is a girl . . ." in *American Poetry Review* (1977);
"for the blind" in *Nimrod* (1977).

for elaine and eileen
who listen

contents

homage to mine

two-headed woman

the light that came to lucille clifton

homage to mine

lucy and her girls

lucy is the ocean
extended by
her girls
are the river
fed by
lucy
is the sun
reflected through
her girls
are the moon
lighted by
lucy
is the history of
her girls
are the place where
lucy
was going

i was born with twelve fingers
like my mother and my daughter.
each of us
born wearing strange black gloves
extra baby fingers hanging over the sides of our cribs and
dipping into the milk.
somebody was afraid we would learn to cast spells
and our wonders were cut off
but they didn't understand
the powerful memory of ghosts.   now
we take what we want
with invisible fingers
and we connect
my dead mother   my live daughter   and me
through our terrible shadowy hands.

homage to my hair

when i feel her jump up and dance
i hear the music! my God
i'm talking about my nappy hair!
she is a challenge to your hand
Black man,
she is as tasty on your tongue as good greens
Black man,
she can touch your mind
with her electric fingers and
the grayer she do get, good God,
the Blacker she do be!

homage to my hips

these hips are big hips.
they need space to
move around in.
they don't fit into little
petty places. these hips
are free hips.
they don't like to be held back.
these hips have never been enslaved,
they go where they want to go
they do what they want to do.
these hips are mighty hips.
these hips are magic hips.
i have known them
to put a spell on a man and
spin him like a top!

what the mirror said

listen,
you a wonder.
you a city
of a woman.
you got a geography
of your own.
listen,
somebody need a map
to understand you.
somebody need directions
to move around you.
listen,
woman,
you not a noplace
anonymous
girl;
mister with his hands on you
he got his hands on
some
damn
body!

there is a girl inside.
she is randy as a wolf.
she will not walk away
and leave these bones
to an old woman.

she is a green tree
in a forest of kindling.
she is a green girl
in a used poet.

she has waited
patient as a nun
for the second coming,
when she can break through gray hairs
into blossom

and her lovers will harvest
honey and thyme
and the woods will be wild
with the damn wonder of it.

to merle

say skinny manysided tall on the ball
brown downtown woman
last time i saw you was on the corner of
pyramid and sphinx.
ten thousand years have interrupted our conversation
but i have kept most of my words
till you came back.
what i'm trying to say is
i recognize your language and
let me call you sister, sister,
i been waiting for you.

august the 12th

for sam

we are two scars on a dead woman's belly
brother, cut from the same knife
you and me. today is your birthday.
where are you? my hair
is crying for her brother.
myself with a mustache
empties the mirror on our mothers' table
and all the phones in august wait.
today is your birthday, call us.
tell us where you are,
tell us why you are silent now.

on the death of allen's son

a certain man had seven sons.
who can fill the space that
one space makes?
young friend, young enemy who bloomed
off his stick like a miracle
who will he find to fish the waters
he had saved for you?
his name stood at attention
in seven letters,
now there are six
and it never again
can be pronounced the same.

speaking of loss

i began with everything;
parents, two extra fingers
a brother to ruin. i was
a rich girl with no money
in a red dress. how did i come
to sit in this house
wearing a name i never heard
until i was a woman? someone has stolen
my parents and hidden my brother.
my extra fingers are cut away.
i am left with plain hands and
nothing to give you but poems.

**to thelma who worried because
i couldn't cook**

because no man would taste you
you tried to feed yourself
kneading your body
with your own fists. the beaten thing
rose up like a dough
and burst in the oven of your hunger.
madam, i'm not your gifted girl,
i am a woman and
i know what to do.

**poem on my fortieth birthday to
my mother who died young**

well i have almost come to the place where you fell
tripping over a wire at the forty-fourth lap
and i have decided to keep running,
head up, body attentive, fingers
aimed like darts at first prize, so
i might not even watch out for the thin thing
grabbing toward my ankles but
i'm trying for the long one mama,
running like hell and if i fall
i fall.

february 13, 1980

twenty-one years of my life you have been
the lost color in my eye. my secret blindness,
all my seeings turned grey with your going.
mother, i have worn your name like a shield.
it has torn but protected me all these years,
now even your absence comes of age.
i put on a dress called woman for this day
but i am not grown away from you
whatever i say.

forgiving my father

it is friday. we have come
to the paying of the bills.
all week you have stood in my dreams
like a ghost, asking for more time
but today is payday, payday old man;
my mother's hand opens in her early grave
and i hold it out like a good daughter.

there is no more time for you. there will
never be time enough daddy daddy old lecher
old liar. i wish you were rich so i could take it all
and give the lady what she was due
but you were the son of a needy father,
the father of a needy son;
you gave her all you had
which was nothing. you have already given her
all you had.

you are the pocket that was going to open
and come up empty any friday.
you were each other's bad bargain, not mine.
daddy old pauper   old prisoner,   old dead man
what am i doing here collecting?
you lie side by side in debtors' boxes
and no accounting will open them up.

to the unborn and waiting children

i went into my mother as
some souls go into a church,
for the rest only. but there,
even there, from the belly of a
poor woman who could not save herself
i was pushed without my permission
into a tangle of birthdays.
listen, eavesdroppers, there is no such thing
as a bed without affliction;
the bodies all may open wide but
you enter at your own risk.

aunt agnes hatcher tells

1. about the war

after the war when rationing was over
was a plenty names. people
shuffled them like cards and drew
new ones out the deck. child,
letters and numbers went
running through whole families.
everybody's cousin was
somebody else. just
consider yourself lucky if
you know who you are.

2. about my mama

your mama, her bottom turned into hamburger
during the war but it was fat meat and
nobody wanted any. she sang jesus keep me and
beat her fists into fits. fell dead
in the hospital hall
two smiles next to the virgin mary.
glad to be gone.
hunger can kill you.
she's how i know.

3. about my daddy

your daddy, he decided to spread the wealth
as they say, and made another daughter.
just before the war she come calling
looking like his natural blood.
your mama surprised us and opened her heart.
none of his other tricks worked that good.

4. about me

you
slavery time they would be calling you
worth your weight in diamonds the way you
slide out babies like payday from that
billion dollar behind.

the once and future dead
who learn they will be white men
weep for their history. we call it
rain.

two-headed woman

in this garden
growing
following strict orders
following the Light
see the sensational
two-headed woman
one face turned outward
one face
swiveling slowly in

the making of poems

the reason why i do it
though i fail and fail
in the giving of true names
is i am adam and his mother
and these failures are my job.

new year

lucy
by sam
out of thelma
limps down a ramp
toward the rest of her life.
with too many candles
in her hair
she is a princess of
burning buildings
leaving the year that
tried to consume her.
her hands are bright
as they witch for water
and even her tears cry
fire   fire
but she opens herself
to the risk of flame and
walks toward an ocean
of days.

sonora desert poem

for lois and richard shelton

1.
the ones who live in the desert,
if you knew them
you would understand everything.
they see it all and
never judge any
just drink the water when
they get the chance.
if i could grow arms on my scars
like them,
if i could learn
the patience they know
i wouldn't apologize for my thorns either
just stand in the desert
and witness.

2.
directions for watching the sun set in the desert

come to the landscape that was hidden under the sea.
look in the opposite direction.
reach for the mountain.
the mountain will ignore your hand.
the sun will fall on your back.
the landscape will fade away.
you will think you're alone until a flash
of green incredible light.

3.
directions for leaving the desert

push the bones back
under your skin.
finish the water.
they will notice your thorns and
ask you to testify.
turn toward the shade.
smile.
say nothing at all.

my friends

no they will not understand
when i throw off my legs and my arms
at your hesitant yes.
when i throw them off and slide
like a marvelous snake toward your bed
your box   whatever you will keep me in
no   they will not understand what can be
so valuable beyond paper dollars diamonds
what is to me worth all appendages.
they will never understand   never approve
of me loving at last where i would
throw it all off to be,
with you   in your small room   limbless
but whole.

wife

we are some of us
born for the water.
we begin at once
swimming toward him.
we sight him.
we circle him like a ring.
if he does not drown us we stay.
if he does
we swim like a fish for his brother.

i once knew a man

i once knew a man who had wild horses killed.
when he told about it
the words came galloping out of his mouth
and shook themselves and headed off in
every damn direction. his tongue
was wild and wide and spinning when he talked
and the people he looked at closed their eyes
and tore the skins off their backs as they walked away
and stopped eating meat.
there was no holding him once he got started;
he had had wild horses killed one time and
they rode him to his grave.

angels

"the angels say they have no wings"

two shining women.
i will not betray you with
public naming
nor celebrate actual birthdays.
you are my two good secrets
lady dark   lady fair.
no one will know that i recognize
the rustle of sky in your voices
and your meticulous absence
of wing.

**conversation with my grandson,
waiting to be conceived**

you will bloom
in a family of flowers.
you are the promise
the Light made to adam,
the love you will grow in
is the garden of Our Lord.

"and i will be a daisy.
daddy too.
mommy is a dandelion. grandma
you are a flower
that has no name."

the mystery that surely is present
as the underside of the leaf
turning to stare at you quietly
from your hand,
that is the mystery you have not
looked for, and it turns
with a silent shattering of your life
for who knows ever after
the proper position of things
or what is waiting to turn from us
even now?

the astrologer predicts at mary's birth

this one lie down on grass.
this one old men will follow
calling Mother   Mother.
she womb will blossom then die.
this one she hide from evening.
at a certain time when she hear something
it will burn her ear.
at a certain place when she see something
it will break her eye.

anna speaks of the childhood
of mary her daughter

we rise up early and
we work. work is the medicine
for dreams.
         that dream
i am having again;
she washed in light,
whole world bowed to its knees,
she on a hill looking up,
face all long tears.
         and shall i give her up
to dreaming then? i fight this thing.
all day we scrubbing   scrubbing.

35

mary's dream

winged women was saying
"full of grace" and like.
was light beyond sun and words
of a name and a blessing.
winged women to only i.
i joined them, whispering
yes.

how he is coming then

like a pot turned on the straw
nuzzled by cows and an old man
dressed like a father. like a loaf
a poor baker sets in the haystack to cool.
like a shepherd who hears in his herding
his mother whisper   my son   my son.

holy night

joseph, i afraid of stars,
their brilliant seeing.
so many eyes. such light.
joseph, i cannot still these limbs,
i hands keep moving toward i breasts,
so many stars. so bright.
joseph, is wind burning from east
joseph, i shine, oh joseph,   oh
illuminated night.

a song of mary

somewhere it being yesterday.
i a maiden in my mother's house.
the animals silent outside.
is morning.
princes sitting on thrones in the east
studying the incomprehensible heavens.
joseph carving a table somewhere
in another place.
i watching my mother.
i smiling an ordinary smile.

island mary

after the all been done and i
one old creature carried on
another creature's back, i wonder
could i have fought these thing?
surrounded by no son of mine save
old men calling Mother like in the tale
the astrologer tell, i wonder
could i have walk away when voices
singing in my sleep? i one old woman.
always i seem to worrying now for
another young girl asleep
in the plain evening.
what song around her ear?
what star still choosing?

mary   mary astonished by God
on a straw bed circled by beasts
and an old husband. mary marinka
holy woman split by sanctified seed
into mother and Mother for ever and ever
we pray for you sister woman shook by the
awe full affection of the Saints.

for the blind

you will enter morning
without error.
you will stand in a room
where you have never lingered.
you will touch glass.
someone will face you with bones
repeating your bones.
you will feel them in the glass.
your fingers will shine
with recognition,
your eyes will open
with delight.

for the mad

you will be alone at last
in the sanity of your friends.

brilliance will fade away from you
and you will settle in dimmed light.

you will not remember how to mourn
your dying difference.

you will not be better but
they will say you are well.

for the lame

happen you will rise,
lift from grounded in a spin
and begin to forget the geography
of fixed things.
happen you will walk past
where you meant to stay,
happen you will wonder at the way
it seemed so marvelous to move.

for the mute

they will blow from your mouth one morning
like from a shook bottle
and you will try to keep them for
tomorrow's conversation but
your patience will be broken when the
bottle bursts
and you will spill all of your
extraordinary hearings for there are
too many languages for
one mortal tongue.

God waits for the wandering world.
He expects us when we enter,
late or soon.
He will not mind my coming after hours.
His patience is His promise.

the light that came to lucille clifton
came in a shift of knowing
when even her fondest sureties
faded away. it was the summer
she understood that she had not understood
and was not mistress even
of her own off eye. then
the man escaped throwing away his tie and
the children grew legs and started walking and
she could see the peril of an
unexamined life.
she closed her eyes, afraid to look for her
authenticity
but the light insists on itself in the world;
a voice from the nondead past started talking,
she closed her ears and it spelled out in her hand
"you might as well answer the door, my child,
  the truth is furiously knocking."

the light that came
to lucille clifton

testament

in the beginning
was the Word.

the year of Our Lord,
amen. i
lucille clifton
hereby testify
that in that room
there was a light
and in that light
there was a voice
and in that voice
there was a sigh
and in that sigh
there was a world.
a world a sigh a voice a light and
i
alone
in a room.

incandescence
formless form
and the soft
shuffle of sound

who are these strangers
peopleing this light?

lucille
we are
the Light

mother, i am mad.
we should have guessed
a twelve-fingered flower
might break. my knowing
flutters to the ground.

mother i have managed to unlearn
my lessons. i am left
in otherness. mother

someone calling itself Light
has opened my inside.
i am flooded with brilliance
mother,

someone of it is answering to
your name.

perhaps

i am going blind.
my eyes exploding,
seeing more than is there
until they burst into nothing

or going deaf, these sounds
the feathered hum of silence

or going away from my self, the cool
fingers of lace on my skin
the fingers of madness

or perhaps
in the palace of time
our lives are a circular stair
and i am turning

explanations

anonymous water can slide under the ground.

the wind can shiver with desire.

this room can settle.

this body can settle.

but can such a sound
cool as a circle
surround and
pray
or promise
or prophesy?

friends come

explaining to me that my mind
is the obvious assassin

the terrorist of voices
who has waited
to tell me miraculous lies
all my life. no

i say
friends
the ones who talk to me
their words thin as wire
their chorus fine as crystal
their truth direct as stone,
they are present as air.

they are there.

to joan

joan
did you never hear
in the soft rushes of france
merely the whisper of french grass
rubbing against leathern
sounding now like a windsong
now like a man?
did you never wonder
oh fantastical joan,
did you never cry in the sun's face
unreal   unreal? did you never run
villageward
hands pushed out toward your apron?
and just as you knew that your mystery
was broken for all time
did they not fall then
soft as always
into your ear
calling themselves Michael
among beloved others?
and you
sister   sister
did you not then sigh
my voices   my voices   of course?

confession

father
i am not equal to the faith required.
i doubt.
i have a woman's certainties;
bodies pulled from me,
pushed into me.
bone flesh is what i know.

father
the angels say they have no wings.
i woke one morning
feeling how to see them.
i could discern their shadows
in the shadow. i am not
equal to the faith required.

father
i see your mother standing now
shoulderless and shoeless by your side.
i hear her whisper truths i cannot know.
father i doubt.

father
what are the actual certainties?
your mother speaks of love.

the angels say they have no wings.
i am not equal to the faith required.
i try to run from such surprising presence;
the angels stream before me
like a torch.

in populated air
our ancestors continue.
i have seen them.
i have heard
their shimmering voices
singing.

THE
JUNIPER
PRIZE

This volume is the sixth recipient
of the Juniper Prize,
presented annually by the
University of Massachusetts Press
for a volume of original poetry.
The prize is named in honor of Robert Francis,
who has lived for many years at
Fort Juniper, Amherst, Massachusetts.

Library of Congress Cataloging in Publication Data
Clifton, Lucille, 1936–
Two-headed woman.
I. Title.
PS3553.L45T8   811'.54   80–5379
ISBN 0–87023–309–2
ISBN 0–87023–310–6 (pbk.)